Share a

by Marilyn Deen

Consultant:
Adria F. Klein, PhD
California State University, San Bernardino

CAPSTONE PRESS
a capstone imprint

Wonder Readers are published by Capstone Press,
1710 Roe Crest Drive, North Mankato, Minnesota 56003.
www.capstonepub.com

Library of Congress Cataloging-in-Publication Data
Deen, Marilyn.
  Share and be fair / Marilyn Deen.—1st ed.
    p. cm.—(Wonder readers)
  Includes index.
  ISBN 978-1-4296-9609-8 (library binding)
  ISBN 978-1-4296-7935-0 (paperback)
  ISBN 978-1-62065-367-8 (ebook PDF)
  1. Sharing in children—Juvenile literature. 2. Fairness—Juvenile literature. I. Title.
  BF723.S428D44 2013
  177.7—dc23   2011022024

Summary: Simple text and color photographs present the concept of division.

Note to Parents and Teachers

The Wonder Readers: Mathematics series supports national mathematics
standards. These titles use text structures that support early readers, specifically
with a close photo/text match and glossary. Each book is perfectly leveled to
support the reader at the right reading level, and the topics are of high interest.
Early readers will gain success when they are presented with a book that is of
interest to them and is written at the appropriate level.

Printed in the United States of America in North Mankato, Minnesota.
042012   006682CGF12

Table of Contents

Fair Sharing 4
Taking Turns 6
Sharing with Others......................10
Splitting Up 14
Glossary...18
Now Try This! 19
Internet Sites 19
Index 20

Fair Sharing

No fair! That's what some people say when they think someone isn't splitting things equally with them. When you **share**, it is important to be **fair**.

You are fair when you make sure everyone gets the same amount of whatever you are sharing. This orange can be cut into slices so everyone can have a taste.

Taking Turns

These three friends want to play a video game. Only two people can play at a time.

The three friends take turns. One friend waits **patiently** for the other friends to finish. Each person can take a turn to play the game.

Three friends want to eat lunch together. But there is only one pizza. They each want their fair share of the pizza.

There are six slices of pizza.
Each person can have two slices.
That is fair sharing. It is also
a yummy lunch!

Sharing with Others

It can be tempting to keep what you have for yourself. Sometimes you don't want to share.

Sharing what you have with others can make you feel good. It can make your friends feel good too. Sharing shows that you care about making another person happy.

These friends are thirsty. They have different drinks to share. If all of the milk is gone, they pick the juice. They know how to make it fair.

These two friends put their money together to pay for a bag of popcorn. They know how to share.

Splitting Up

Sometimes it is easy to share and be fair because there is just enough for each person. Sometimes it is not so easy. These three friends want to swing, but there are only two swings. That makes it harder to share and be fair.

Sometimes you have to split things
up in order to share them. These two
friends want to share one apple.
By cutting the apple in **half**,
they can share and be fair.

This brother and sister each want
to watch a different TV program.
They **decide** to share the remote.
That would be fair.

It feels good when things are fair.
It also feels good to share.
What are other ways you can
share and be fair?

Glossary

decide	to make up your mind
fair	equal or even
half	one of two equal parts of something
patiently	staying calm without getting angry or upset
share	to let someone else have part of something you have

Now Try This!

With a group of friends, look for classroom items, such as paper clips, pencils, and rulers, to divide among yourselves. Use the division problems solved in this book as examples.

Internet Sites

FactHound offers a safe, fun way to find Internet sites related to this book. All of the sites on FactHound have been researched by our staff.

Here's all you do:

Visit *www.facthound.com*

Type in this code: 9781429696098

Super-cool stuff! Check out projects, games and lots more at www.capstonekids.com

Index

caring, 11

deciding, 16

fairness, 4–5, 8–9, 12, 14, 15, 16, 17

half, 15

money, 13

playing, 6–7

sharing, 4–5, 8–9, 10–11, 12, 13, 14, 15, 16, 17

slices, 5, 9

splitting, 4, 15

taking turns, 7

Editorial Credits

Maryellen Gregoire, project director; Mary Lindeen, consulting editor; Gene Bentdahl, designer; Sarah Schuette, editor; Wanda Winch, media researcher; Eric Manske, production specialist

Photo Credits

All images by Capstone Studio: Karon Dubke

Word Count: **356**   Guided Reading Level: **J**   Early Intervention Level: **16**